A PORTRAIT OF
YORK

IAN CARSTAIRS

HALSGROVE

First published in Great Britain in 2004

Copyright © 2004 text and photographs Ian Carstairs

Title page photograph: Metal Rose – City Walls, Micklegate Bar.

British Library Cataloguing-in-Publication Data
A CIP record for this title is available from the British Library

ISBN 1 84114 382 0

HALSGROVE
Halsgrove House
Lower Moor Way
Tiverton, Devon EX16 6SS
Tel: 01884 243242
Fax: 01884 243325
email: sales@halsgrove.com
website: www.halsgrove.com

Printed and bound by D'Auria Industrie Grafiche Spa, Italy

ACKNOWLEDGEMENTS
The photographs of York Minster on pages 113–117 are © Dean and Chapter of York: by kind permission/Ian Carstairs;
those on pages 9–11, 123, 126 and 127, are courtesy of the National Railway Museum, Monks Cross Shopping Park,
Yorkshire Museum of Farming and Yorkshire Air Museum respectively.
Thanks are also due to Archer Carstairs, for his patient assistance with this project.

Introduction

If there is one city in England capable of demanding our attention, pulling our thoughts in different directions, stimulating our moods and thrilling our senses all at the same time, then the city of York must surely be it.

With almost-intact medieval walls surrounding its ancient heart, York is a city on a human scale, which somehow wraps itself around you and which for many, never lets you go. Most importantly, it boasts a first-class public transport system, where the automobile is being put in its place and the streets given back to the people.

Here, straddling the River Ouse, lay a great centre for Romans, Anglo-Saxons and Vikings, which in Victorian times became a hub for the development of railways, the forerunner of today's worldwide tourism.

We can only wonder what it was like here in the past and purely guess at the awe which the almost unbelievable scale of York Minster must have evoked in ordinary people across the centuries. Even now, from tens of kilometres away, its massive shape still stands as the defining feature of the city within the wide low-lying lands of its eponymous vale.

Today, the modern city of York extends well beyond the ancient heart, and dramatic new buildings have come to play a part in the quality of the landscape and street scene.

Creating this portrait of York has been a fascinating task. It would have been tempting to focus solely on its historic places, but that would have been to ignore the fact that this is not just 'Heritage Land', but also a thriving, varied and modern city, with some remarkable countryside too.

My photographs, mostly taken unashamedly as grabbed moments on shopping trips, after business meetings or on days out, reflect the things I like or have noticed; many are obvious, others a little more obscure. Taking them encouraged me to look harder, not just at the famous attractions, but at the shapes of buildings, at their roofscapes, the play of light and at the not-so-glamorous structures which are nevertheless distinctive of their eras. Most significant of all, it caused me to look up above the eye-level at the details of facades, which I had never previously noticed: I found I saw everything with 'new eyes'.

I hope this selection will lead and encourage you, not only to discover your own surprises, but perhaps also to experience the familiar anew.

Ian Carstairs, 2004

The City of York

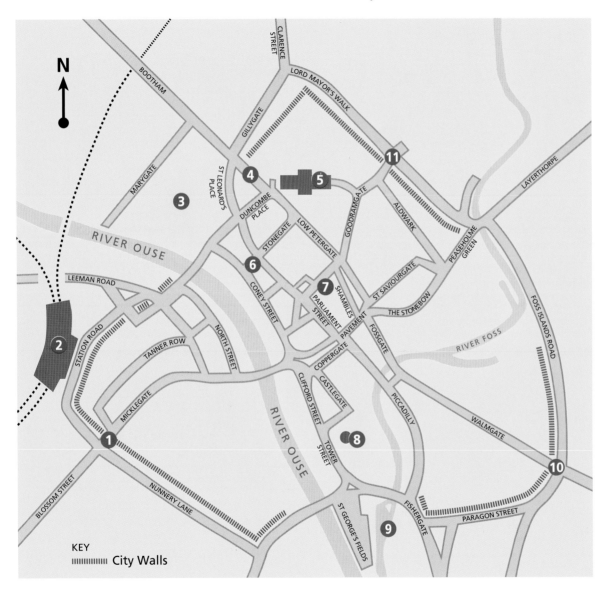

1 Micklegate Bar
2 York Railway Station
3 Museum Gardens
4 Bootham Bar
5 York Minster
6 Mansion House
7 Newgate Market
8 Clifford's Tower
9 Foss Basin
10 Walmgate Bar
11 Monk Bar

KEY
|||||||||| City Walls

Spring in York
Thousands of daffodils blanketing the ramparts of the historic medieval defences herald
the beginning of spring, as well as the start of York's main tourist season.

Micklegate Bar

Dating from the twelfth century, Micklegate Bar, historically the most important of York's gateways, was also the place where the heads of traitors were put on display.

The City of York
Walking the walls from Micklegate Bar in early evening offers a stunning view towards York Minster.

York Railway Station – Station Road
Arguably, one of the great Victorian buildings of England, York Station was considered to be the
largest station in the world when completed in the late 1870s.

**Royal decoration – National Railway
Museum – Leeman Road**
Decorations used for Royal trains on the London
Brighton and South Coast Railway are displayed
on the 1882 locomotive *Gladstone* – named
after the Prime Minister of the time – at
the turntable in the main hall of the largest
railway museum in the world.

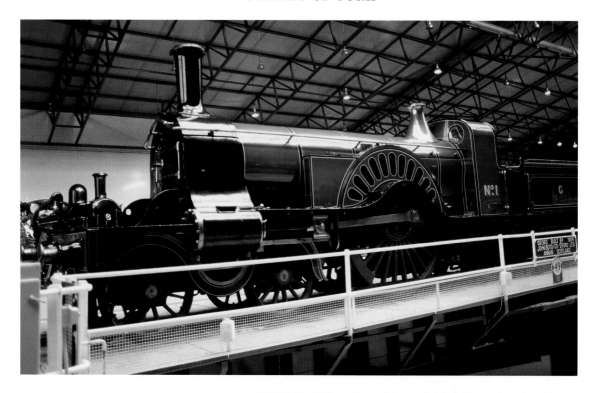

Stirling 4-2-2 (top)
A 'Stirling Single' as it is known, after its designer and the large single-axle driving wheels, on the turntable provides a dramatic centre-piece to the museum's extensive collections.

An early train (right)
A cut-away replica of Stephenson's *Rocket* (1829) heads Liverpool and Manchester Railway carriages, the design of which was based on a road stage-coach with a railway chassis. At the opening of the railway, Liverpool MP William Huskisson misjudged *Rocket's* speed and he became the first rail fatality.

Flying Scotsman comes home
Built in Doncaster, Yorkshire in 1923, the most famous steam locomotive in the world is welcomed to the National Railway Museum.
Saved for the nation by support from the National Heritage Memorial Fund in memory of those who have given
their lives for the United Kingdom, people simply adore her.

Old North Eastern Railway headquarters – Station Road
Facing the original Victorian station, this distinctive red and white building was formerly the headquarters of the
North Eastern Railway Company (1906–1923), then of respective successor railway companies over the years.

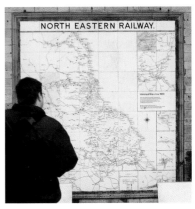

Door arch – NER building
An intricate carving over a doorway records the building's association with the
North Eastern Railway (NER) whose extensive routes at the beginning of the
twentieth century can be seen on a tile map (right) in York Station concourse.

Cholera burial ground – Station Road
Some of the 185 victims of the summer 1882 cholera epidemic lie
in a special burial ground, outside the city walls.

37 Tanner Row
Formerly a hotel to serve the city's early Victorian railway station, number 37 is now home to the Yorkshire Regional Headquarters of English Heritage, the Government organisation with special responsibility for historic buildings and ancient monuments.

Barker Tower – North Street
A chain once linked Barker Tower with a similar structure, now part of Lendal Tower, on the opposite bank of the River Ouse. Normally the chain lay on the riverbed, but could be raised in times of tension to help defend the city from incursions along the river.

River Ouse
A boat trip on the River Ouse, which drains the Yorkshire Dales and Vale of York into the Humber Estuary,
offers a relaxing way to enjoy the city and its surroundings.

Old and new – Marygate

Westgate apartments, an impressive new development, adds a powerful quality to the roofscape of the north of the city and with its circular atriums and square tower-like shape is not unsympathetic with its historic surroundings.

Multangular tower – Museum Gardens
The Roman multangular tower, which formed the north-west corner of the Roman fortress,
was later incorporated into the medieval city walls. The larger blocks of stone
at the higher levels are the later work.

Overleaf: **Yorkshire Museum – Museum Gardens**
With a fine range of exhibits including the exquisite Middleham Jewel, the Yorkshire Museum
holds one of the country's premier regional collections.

St Mary's Abbey – Museum Gardens
Founded in the eleventh century, the monastery was destroyed by Henry VIII during the Dissolution of the Monasteries in 1539.

St Mary's Abbey
William Rufus, son of King William, laid
the foundation stone for the original abbey
church in 1088. This was rebuilt in the
thirteenth century and its remains form
the romantic ruins we see today.

Hospitium – Museum Gardens
Formerly the guest hall of St Mary's Abbey, this much-restored building
is one the oldest timbered structures in York.

York Observatory – Museum Gardens
The observatory, a gem born of the early nineteenth century quest for knowledge, was built by
York Philosophical Society in 1831, in an era before the depressing impact of light pollution.

The Red House – Duncombe Place
An early eighteenth century house built for the then Lord Mayor of York, Sir William Robinson. It is more likely that it takes its name from being constructed in part from red brick, rather than from the colour it is painted.

York Theatre Royal – St Leonard's Place
York's premier performance venue is a curious mixture of building styles.

De Grey Rooms – St Leonard's Place
Named after Archbishop Walter De Grey who initiated the building of the present York Minster,
the early Victorian buildings of 1841 now house the Tourist Information Centre.

King's Manor – Exhibition Square
Before St Mary's Abbey was dissolved in 1539, King's Manor was the abbot's lodgings.
Now occupied by the University of York, it reflects a mixture of building and maintenance work
over many centuries. King Charles I's coat-of-arms is displayed above the ancient doorway.

Art Gallery – Exhibition Square

A range of paintings depicting the development of European portraiture, including an unforgettable masterpiece
of Jean Abercrombie by Scottish painter Allan Ramsey (1713–1784), is a centrepiece of the gallery's collections.

Bootham Bar
The northern gateway of the medieval city, formerly had a barbican – additional external defences – but like those on all but one of the main entrances, Walmgate Bar, it has been demolished.

Exhibition Square
A popular place to board the buses on which visitors can enjoy a guided tour of the city.

Exhibition Square
The statue of William Etty RA surveys one of England's great historic city scenes.

St Peter's School – Bootham
Founded by Paulinus in AD627, St Peter's
names among its old boys one the most infamous
characters in English history – Guy Fawkes –
who allegedly conspired to blow-up the
Houses of Parliament in 1605.

**Fountains Learning Centre,
St John's College – Clarence Street**
Completed in 2003, the centre is also home to
the celebrated Yorkshire Film Archive, containing a
large collection of historic film footage taken across
the region, which is accessible to the public.

River Foss – Foss Islands Bridge
No city walls were needed in the area between Peasholme Green and the Red Tower, which in medieval times was a large pool.

Old County Hospital – Foss Islands Bridge
When 'The County' closed as a hospital it was turned into offices and subsequently apartments.

York Old Power Station – Foss Islands Road
All that remains of an electricity generating
station (there once was an accompanying cooling
tower) the chimney, which is an historic
listed building, still bears faint evidence
of Second World War camouflage.

Gas Holder – Layerthorpe
Once a feature of every town, gas holders largely became redundant with the advent of natural gas.
Should this fine example ever be lost, we will have been deprived of an important part of our heritage,
intimately connected with the way in which modern cities developed.

Red Tower – Foss Islands Road
The only tower in the city walls to be constructed of brick, it marks the end of the pool
and the transition back to the stone defences. The use of brick lightened the structure,
which might otherwise have been unstable being built in a wet area.

Walmgate Bar – Walmgate
The only city gateway to retain its barbican – an outer secondary defence for the gate.
The wooden house built inside the Bar was added in Elizabethan times.

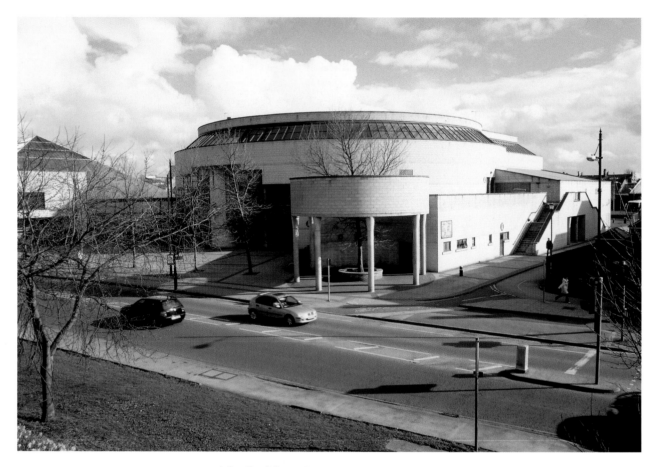

The Barbican Centre – Paragon Street
Widely opposing views surround the possible redevelopment of this performance centre, which along with the adjacent swimming baths is located on the former site of York livestock market.

Tree – Paragon Street
A curious place to put a tree – visible in the small circular feature in front of the Barbican Centre (opposite).

York City Walls – Paragon Street
A walk round the city walls is a highlight of any visit to York. Dating in part from as early as Roman times though mostly of medieval construction, they are a defining feature of this unique city.

City Walls – Fishergate
An elevated position in the corner tower above Fishergate offers a vantage point for the view down towards
Fishergate Postern Tower, Castle Mills and the Castle Museum.

Travelodge and the Posterngate
New buildings, sympathetically designed without trying to replicate the historic structures
which surround them, make a refreshing contribution to the street scene.

Fishergate Postern Tower
Historically the area around Castle Mills was
a great pool controlled by a dam in the River
Foss, with Fishergate Postern Tower standing
in the edge of the water. Almost 500 years
old, it has remained unchanged, except
for its roof, which used to be flat.

Raindale Mill – Castle Mills Bridge
Moved stone-by-stone from Raindale in the North York Moors, the mill is in working order
and open to visitors to the Castle Museum during the summer.

Foss Barrier – St George's Fields car park
York's flood defences include a barrier across the mouth of the River Foss basin. In times of high flood risk,
the barrier is closed within the arched glazed structure to prevent the Ouse backing up into the Foss.

Foss Basin footbridge – St George's Fields car park
An attractive wrought-iron, hand-cranked lifting-bridge, spanning the entrance to the Foss Basin,
could be raised to allow vessels into the River Foss.

Millennium Bridge – Fulford to Clementhorpe
A modern structure, built as its name suggests to commemorate the end of the second millennium,
enables an attractive circular walk south of the city to be completed using both banks of the river.

Skeldergate Bridge
The most southerly of York's
three city road bridges required
the removal of parts of the medieval
defences when it was built in 1882.

Skeldergate Bridge
Since the construction of a weir in 1757 at Naburn to maintain a depth upstream for navigation, the River Ouse
ceased to be tidal through York. However, it is still open to through navigation via a lock
which enables vessels to negotiate the obstacle.

85–89 Micklegate
This significant group of buildings dating from perhaps the late fifteenth century, stands between the site of the now demolished gateway to a medieval priory – Priory Street – and the site of the Priory Church.

Micklegate House – Micklegate
Built in 1752 by John Carr for John Bourchier of Beningborough Hall, this imposing Georgian residence
with many attractive interior features is a splendid location for York Backpackers' Hostel.

All Saints' Church – North Street
The slender spire to the west of the
River Ouse marks this beautiful medieval
church, containing craftsmanship
of the highest quality.

Ouse Bridge
Started in 1810, Ouse Bridge was completed in 1821 at which time it was a toll bridge.
Within ten years its use had become free of charge.

Overleaf: **Winter Flood – Ouse Bridge**
Winter floods are a common occurrence in York, though are now largely contained by extensive flood defence
and alleviation works both in the city and upstream.

King's Arms – King's Staith
Renowned for being regularly flooded – a depth of up to two metres is not unheard of – the relationship between the pub and the river is always a source of fascination.

River Ouse – Ouse Bridge
The River Ouse, back in its banks, was the lifeblood for trade for the city in historic times.
Today it is used mostly for recreation and as a feature for many new riverside developments.

Cumberland House – King's Staith
An imposing riverside house, thought to
have been named after George II's son,
the Duke of Cumberland, upon whom
was bestowed the Freedom of the City
on his return journey to London after
his victory at the Battle of
Culloden in 1746.

Clifford's Tower – Tower Street
Built in the thirteenth century to replace a wooden keep constructed on the mound during the reign of
William the Conqueror, the tower is unparalleled and offers a classic view across the city.

Clifford's Tower
In the often grim annals of history, the tower has its own terrible events to record. In 1190, the Jews of York
committed mass suicide here when given the choice between being baptised or killed. The tower,
which at the time was made from wood, was then burned down.

Opposite: **York city centre – Clifford's Tower**
The 360-degree panorama across the rooftops of York is surpassed only by the 90-mile vista from the top of York Minster's tower.

Castle Museum – Tower Street
Housed in two sections of the eighteenth century prison – here the female prison – the museum is renowned
for its collections from everyday-life including Kirkgate, a re-creation of a cobbled Victorian street.

Castle Museum – the Debtors' Prison
The 'Eye of York' is framed on three sides
by the museum – formerly the Female Prison
and Debtors' Prison – and the Court House.
Clifford's Tower dominates the remaining side.

York Crown Court – Tower Street
A reflection shows part of the former York Castle, which today houses the Crown Court.

Crown Court
Built to a design by John Carr in the 1770s, the façade of the Crown Court is topped by the
figure of Justice with scales and a spear above the entrance.

A show of strength – Clifford Street
A passing wit is caught pretending to lift an escape turntable fire appliance off the ground.
(It is actually on hydraulic jacks out of sight behind a wall.)

Ryedale Building – Piccadilly
The marked contrast between 1960s structures, such as Ryedale Building, and both the historic and recent
architecture raises the question as to whether these buildings are eyesores or valid representatives of their time.

York St Mary's – Castlegate
Now redundant, the former St Mary's Church
has been given a new lease of life as an
exhibition centre explaining York's story.

Opposite, above and below:
Fairfax House – Castlegate
Once the home of Viscount Fairfax in the 1750s,
by the first half of the twentieth century Fairfax
House had declined to use as a cinema and
dance hall. Bought by the York Civic Trust
in the 1980s and fully restored, its exquisite
furnishings open a window into the lives of
the wealthy in Georgian England.

York Magistrates' Court – Clifford Street
The roof of York Magistrates' Court strikes an
unusual pattern – slightly reminiscent, on a tiny
scale, of the domes in the Moscow skyline.

19 Clifford Street
What better place for a solicitor's
office than opposite the magistrates'
court? Buildings are not only
listed for their outside appearance,
but also for other details of their
construction and fittings, such
as the ceilings.

Jorvic Viking Centre – Coppergate Centre
Extensive archaeological remains of Viking York were discovered during excavations for the foundations of the
Coppergate Centre. The world-famous Jorvic Centre – with its equally famous queues – lets you take
a step back in time to witness the sights, smells and sounds of Viking York.

Opposite: **Coney Street**
One of York's main shopping streets, Coney Street is home to a wide range of shops.

Coney Street – above eye-level
Going about our daily lives, we usually only look up a few degrees above eye-level, and without a special effort
it is easy to miss an enormous amount of interest and variety in the shape and details of buildings.

Time the Healer – Coney Street
The large originally seventeenth century clock, adorned by Father Time and a naval officer using a sextant, was badly damaged in 1942 by a Second World War bomb, which destroyed a large part of the adjacent St Martin-le-Grand Church to which it is attached.

River Ouse – Boardwalk
Reached from a passageway alongside St Martin-le-Grand Church – home to some fine medieval stained glass
– the modern boardwalk provides an attractive vantage point to view York's riverscape.

Norwich Union Building – North Street
The detailed design, with complex shapes and dark and slightly mysterious windows,
gives a certain monastic feel to the Norwich Union building.

Overleaf: **River Ouse**
Looking upstream from the east bank boardwalk, the view sweeps from the elegant spire of All Saints' Church,
North Street, past the Norwich Union Building and on to Lendal Bridge.

River Ouse in winter – Ouse Bridge
Upstream from Ouse Bridge, York's first large modern hotel – known formerly as 'The Viking'
and now The Moat House – has become part of the city's built history.

Guildhall – St Helen's Square
Reached through a passageway at the right
of the Mansion House, the original fifteenth
century Guildhall was badly damaged in an
air raid during the Second World War,
though it has since been reconstructed.

Overleaf: **Parliament Street – December**
Christmas in York City Centre is a wonderful
time, with street traders, visiting markets,
colourful attractions, complex decorations
and the enthusiastic bustle of shoppers.

Public toilets – Parliament Street
An extraordinary design, chosen by public vote, delivers a rather grandiose structure on the outside,
which is not quite matched by the design of the facilities inside.

All Saints – Pavement
Partly demolished to enlarge the Market Place and for street-widening, All Saints nevertheless retains another
of York's great features, its octangular lantern tower, once used for hanging a lamp to guide travellers.

**Sir Thomas Herbert's House
– Pavement**
The home of the Herbert family from
the mid-to-late sixteenth century, the
block of buildings stretches back down
Lady Peckett's Yard. When viewed from
the upper floor windows of the building
opposite, detailed carvings, almost unseen
from the ground, can be appreciated.

Lady Peckett's Yard
A short alleyway running under the right hand corner
of Sir Thomas Herbert's House and linking to a little
lane to Fossgate, is named after Alice Peckett, wife of
John Peckett, Lord Mayor of York in 1701.

Entrance – Fossgate
York is famous for its passages and alleyways, popularly
known as 'snickleways'. Through this colourful entrance
lies one of the gems of medieval York.

Merchant Adventurers' Hall – Piccadilly
Built between 1357 and 1361, the hall is one of the finest medieval guildhalls in Europe. The stone chapel at the southern end
was rebuilt in 1411, possibly re-using stone from an earlier period. The Great Room is virtually unaltered.

Merchant Adventurers' Hall
The extensive timbers and free-standing nature of the hall make this an ideal building for appreciating
the way in which timber-framed buildings were constructed.

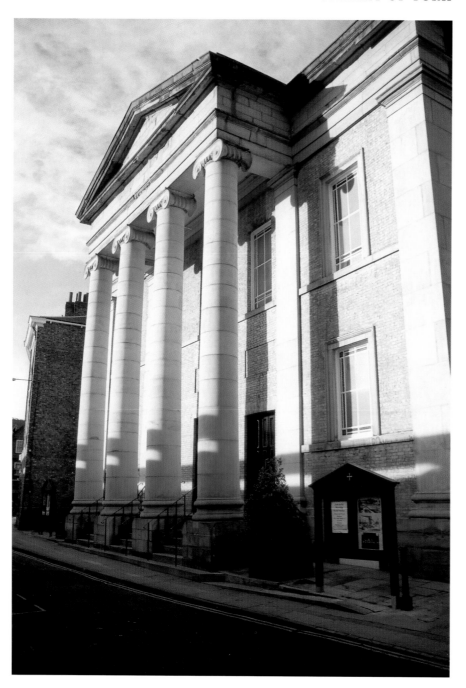

Central Methodist Church – St Saviourgate
The colossal columns of this early
Victorian building, which is capable of
accommodating more than 1000 people,
contrast markedly with neighbouring
properties in this confined street,
where their scale and splendour are
difficult to fully appreciate.

Saviourgate Unitarian Chapel – St Saviourgate
What looks right, is right – the 300-year-old chapel is a delightfully understated building.

Hilary House – St Saviour's Place
A utilitarian building, home to the local office of the Inland Revenue, is seemingly totally
out of place with its neighbours. But does it have its own particular value, telling us
something about society's approach to building design at that time?

Stonebow House – Stonebow
Dating from the early 1960s, Stonebow House, sitting on its car park 'plinth',
has a character which can begin to grow on you.

Black Swan public house – Peaseholme Green
A street-trader heads for his pitch on a winter's afternoon past the heavily-timbered fifteenth century Black Swan,
once the childhood home of the mother of General James Wolfe, the hero of Quebec.

17–19 Aldwark
Built around 1720 and incorporating parts
of earlier structures, these dramatically-lit houses forge
a strong presence in the residential street scene.

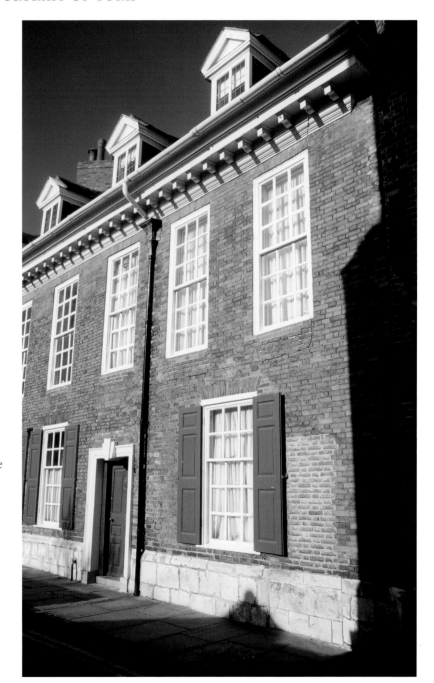

Shambles
York's most famous street, in which some buildings date from the mid-fourteenth century, is named after the 'shammels', the sturdy shelves used by butchers on their shop fronts to display their meat.

Shambles

The Shambles is renowned for the fact that its residents were supposed to be able to shake hands with their neighbours across the street.

4 Jubbergate

This much-restored medieval building standing in a prominent position amid the market was once part
of a longer row of properties. It was left isolated when its neighbours were demolished.
Jubbergate derives its name from 'the street of the British in the Jewish Quarter'.

Newgate Market
York's market is a hive of activity with fruit
and vegetable, fish and cheese stalls and
a wide range of other goods for sale.

York Minster – east end – College Street
A long-term rolling-programme of restoration means the Minster is rarely free of scaffolding these days.
The great east window is the size of a tennis court. It was removed during the Second World War
to protect it from possible bomb damage.

St William's College – College Street
Built in the 1460s, the college has had many uses, including that of the Royal Mint for Charles I during the Civil War.
Today its attractive rooms are excellent venues to hold a meeting or event.

Treasurer's House – Little College Street
Lying behind the Minster, the house, which was
built on the site of the Roman fortress, was the
home of the Minster's treasurer until 1547.

45–51 Goodramgate

This row in Goodramgate, originally named Gutherangate, exhibits a varied range of upper façades and timber-work.
Some of the properties are among the 50 or so in the care of the York Conservation Trust.

64–72 Goodramgate
Lady Row, dating from the early fourteenth century, comprises a range of the
oldest houses in York and perhaps even in the United Kingdom.

63–75 Goodramgate
Opposite Lady Row yet seven centuries apart, an infill replacement building contrasts
markedly with the architecture of its historic neighbours.

York Minster – Duncombe Place
Built between 1220 and 1472, the present Minster is the fourth on the site and is the largest Gothic cathedral north of the Alps.

Opposite: **Minster – west towers**
During the 1970s York Minster was cleaned from top-to-bottom, transforming it from a dark, grimy shape to the startlingly-bright hues shown by its Magnesian limestone.

Minster– south transept

Completed by 1260, the south transept houses the legendary Rose window (c.1500). The world was shocked when, in 1984,
lightning started a fire which destroyed the roof and severely damaged the window, shattering it into more
than 40,000 pieces. They have now been painstakingly restored.

Minster – great west window
Backlit by evening light, the elaborate west window
offers a large, stunning full-stop to the long view
down the length of the nave.

Minster – nave
Completed by the 1350s. It is hard to gain a
true sense of scale in this colossal space when
the nave is empty of chairs and people.

Minster – central tower
The architectural and building skills of fifteenth-century craftsmen are nowhere more
amply demonstrated than looking up inside the Minster's central tower.

Overleaf: **Minster – view east from the central tower**
High above street-level, on a clear day you are rewarded with a spectacular view stretching to the highest part of
the North York Moors, the Yorkshire Dales and the Wolds (on the horizon), and the city and its outskirts.
Some of the varied features of these areas are shown on the following pages, 118 to 131.

York Racecourse – The Knavesmire (4 kms south)
One of the foremost racecourses in the country. On winter days, York's grandstands, set in a wide space,
have a majestic air, like a great ocean-liner at sea.

Opposite: **Bishopthorpe Palace (6 kms south)**
The Gatehouse to Bishopthorpe Palace, the private residence of the Archbishop of York.

Poppleton Sugar Beet Factory (3 kms north-west)
The white plume from the Poppleton chimney and the sweet smell of sugar beet being processed, wafting downwind over tens of kilometres, are a winter-long feature of the city and its surrounding area.

Chocolate Factory – Haxby Road (1 km north)
York's other smell – that of chocolate being made – identifies this as the home of some
of Rowntree's, and later Nestlé's, well-known brands, such as Kit-Kat.

Strensall Common (7 kms north-east)
Occupation by the Ministry of Defence for troop training has helped to retain the character of this
ancient common, a nationally-important area for wildlife, especially insects.

Monks Cross Shopping Park (3 kms north-east)
Out-of-town shopping parks, such as Monks Cross, are popular shopping venues and host many
well-known retailers in a convenient grouping of modern buildings.

**From the electricity supply station
– Osbaldwick (4 kms east)**
Enormous pylons carry electricity supply to and
from this junction of the electricity supply system.
Ugly they may be (though surprisingly not to
everyone) they remind us that we cannot separate
energy-supply infrastructure from life in the city –
without which of course, it could not function.

Park-and-ride – Grimston Bar (4 kms east)
The only sane way to travel into the centre of York, unless you are walking, biking or arriving by train, is to use the park-and-ride system. Grimston Bar is one of several such facilities encircling the city.

Yorkshire Museum of Farming – Murton (5 kms east)
Amid a varied array of historic agricultural implements and practices, there is a reconstruction of a late
Viking settlement, which gives a strong impression of what village life was like 1000 years ago.

Airborne Icons – Yorkshire Air Museum, Elvington (12 kms south-east)

Remarkably, only thirteen years separate the maiden flights of the Handley Page Halifax (*top*) and the Handley Page Victor (*bottom*) which first flew in 1939 and 1952, respectively. The Halifax, named 'Friday the thirteenth' and the only complete reconstruction of the type in the world, is shown at the moving ceremony in May 2004 when the aircraft was dedicated to all the allied air and ground crews that served on Halifaxes. The Victor, one of the three nuclear 'V' bombers of the 1950s, ended its service as an airborne refuelling tanker.

Haytime on the Derwent Ings – Wheldrake (12 kms south-east)
Lying on the city boundary, the 1000-hectare/2470-acre traditionally-farmed
Derwent Ings (a Norse word for seasonally-flooded meadows), is internationally
important for its plants and birds.

Opposite: **Bank Island – Wheldrake (12 kms south-east)**
Winter flood-water transforms the Derwent Ings into a vast 15 kilometre/9
mile-long lake, and the home for thousands of wildfowl and wading birds
which can be viewed from public hides.

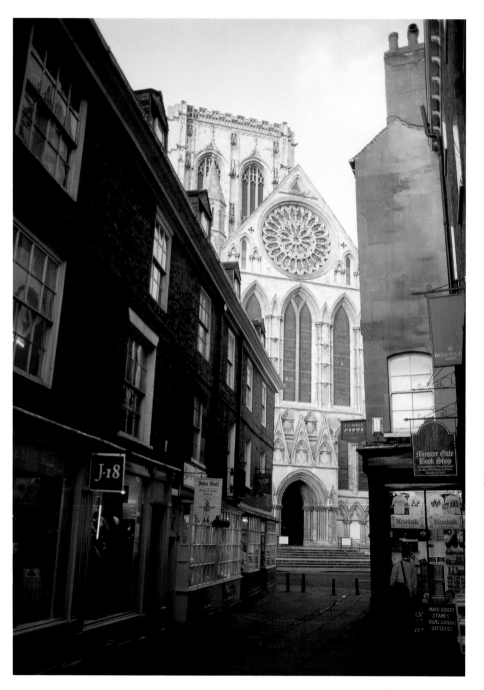

Roman Road – Minster Gates
Down from the tower of the Minster, the
route of the Roman Road from the
river to the fortress followed the present-day
Stonegate and Minster Gates. It was also
the route by which stone was dragged from
barges on the river, to build the Minster.

Previous: **University of York –
Heslington (3 kms south-east)**
Central Hall and University Lake
are at the heart of this popular and
highly-successful university.

Minerva – High Petergate
A carving of Minerva, the Roman Goddess of Wisdom, looks down from the corner of a shop at the junction of High Petergate and Minster Gates, which was formerly a renowned bookshop.

Marking-time – Stonegate
Opposite Minerva, a carved shop corner-post recounts the date of its construction.

Low Petergate
An historic street-scene in Low Petergate, named after St Peter, to whom York Minster is dedicated.

Previous: **Mr Yellow – Low Petergate**
Mr Yellow entertains, amuses and bemuses passing shoppers with his
motionless yet colourful performance.

A traditional shop – Low Petergate
Scott's the Pork Butchers is one of York's popular traditional shops.

Ghostly location – Low Petergate
York is claimed to be one of the most haunted cities in Europe. At night, its
alleyways are the natural home to the supernatural. The spirit of Alice Smith is
said to frequent the passageway where she lived until 1825, when she was
hanged at York Castle, solely for being 'mad.'

Stonegate

Stonegate was the *Via Praetoria* of Roman York, leading to the main gate of the fortress which once stood at the site of the Minster. Its wide variety of buildings and businesses make it one of the most thriving historic streets for shoppers.

15–19 Stonegate, Mulberry Hall
Originally a private house when built in early 1400s, it has been used as a shop for the last
300 years. With its lovely Tudor front, Mulberry Hall is a truly memorable building.

10 and 35 Stonegate

Contrasting wood, tile and pargeting work on the façades make for a complex street scene,
which despite the stark differences still unite to create an overall sense of completeness.

Stonegate
A wet night in mid-winter.

Betty's Tearooms – St Helen's Square
'Betty's' is a renowned place to which to retire after a long day's sightseeing

Mansion House – St Helen's Square
A focus of civic pride for a great city, the Mansion House is an example of early Georgian architecture dating
from 1732, and is the home to the Lord Mayor during his or her year in office.